Animals Growing Up™

HOW PANDAS GROW UP

Lisa Idzikowski

Enslow Publishing
101 W. 23rd Street
Suite 240
New York, NY 10011
USA
enslow.com

WORDS TO KNOW

cub A baby panda.

den The place where panda cubs are born.

habitat A place where animals live.

mammal An animal that has a backbone and hair; females usually give birth to live babies and produce milk to feed their young.

mate The partner an animal chooses to have babies with.

nutrient A substance a body needs to be healthy.

predator An animal that kills other animals for food.

scent A smell.

solitary Living alone.

sow A female giant panda.

CONTENTS

BABY PANDAS

Baby pandas are black, white, and furry. People love to see them at zoos. In nature, these rare bears live in the wild mountains of central China.

FAST FACT

Baby pandas are called cubs.

A panda cub may look cute, but it is still a wild animal.

HABITAT

Giant pandas live in cool, misty mountain forests. They like forests of large, tall trees filled with bamboo. In this habitat, they find all they need to live and grow.

FAST FACT

Panda cubs are able to climb trees by about six months old.

A panda cub is safe from danger far up in a tree.

CUBS ARE BORN

A mother panda settles into her den in a hollowed-out tree or cave. She gives birth to a pink, hairless cub. It cannot see or walk. But it sure squeaks and squawks!

A female giant panda is called a sow.

A newborn panda cub is pink and helpless.

PANDAS ARE MAMMALS

Giant pandas are mammals. A panda sow nurses her cub, or feeds it milk. The milk has special nutrients in it that help the cub fight off disease.

FAST FACT

A panda cub has nothing but mother's milk until about six months old.

A panda cub nurses from its mother.

IN THE DEN

In the den, a mother panda's job is never done. She holds, licks, and feeds her baby. Safe and warm, the cub eats, sleeps, and quickly grows.

A panda sow cleans her cub.

SOLITARY ANIMALS

Giant pandas are solitary animals. They live alone in thick bamboo forests, except when sows have cubs. Pandas also come together in the spring to find a mate.

FAST FACT

Some scientists think that the colors of a panda's coat help keep it hidden.

A panda mother and cub cuddle together in the forest.

15

WHO'S THERE?

Grown-up pandas are quiet most of the time. But they have a way of letting others know they're around. Pandas leave their scent, or smell, everywhere. This scent means, "Here I am!"

A panda cub can smell another panda's scent.

AN UNCOMMON BEAR

Pandas are bears. But unlike other bears, pandas eat almost no meat. Giant pandas eat different types of bamboo, a kind of tall plant. They eat about 30 pounds (14 kilograms) every day.

A panda's teeth marks can tell it apart from others, like a fingerprint.

A panda munches on bamboo leaves.

BE CAREFUL!

A mother panda guards her cub from danger. As **predators**, snow leopards may attack cubs or young pandas. Full grown pandas are too big for most predators.

A mother panda protects her cub.

ALL GROWN UP

Panda cubs do not grow up with brothers and sisters. Cubs live with their mothers until about one and a half years old. They follow her around and learn how to live on their own.

A one-year-old cub (*right*) is almost as big as its mother!

FAST FACT

Panda cubs live with their mothers until about one and a half years old.

LEARN MORE

Books

Anderson, Annmarie. *Giant Pandas*. Washington, DC: Scholastic Nonfiction, 2016.

Richmond, Ben. *Baby Panda Chews Bamboo*. New York, NY: Sterling Children's Books, 2018.

Schuh, Mari. *Giant Pandas*. North Mankato, MN: Capstone Press, 2017.

Websites

National Geographic Kids: Giant Panda
kids.nationalgeographic.com/animals/giant-panda/#giant-panda-eating.jpg
Learn all about pandas.

San Diego Zoo Kids: Giant Panda
kids.sandiegozoo.org/animals/giant-panda
Read fun facts about pandas.

INDEX

Published in 2019 by Enslow Publishing, LLC.
101 W. 23rd Street, Suite 240, New York, NY 10011

Library of Congress Cataloging-in-Publication Data

Names: Idzikowski, Lisa, author.
Title: How pandas grow up / Lisa Idzikowski.
Description: New York, NY : Enslow Publishing, 2019. | Series: Animals growing up | Includes bibliographical references and index. | Audience: Grades K to 3.
Identifiers: LCCN 2017046599| ISBN 9780766096554 (library bound) | ISBN 9780766096561 (pbk.) | ISBN 9780766096578 (6 pack)
Subjects: LCSH: Giant panda—Juvenile literature. | Giant panda—Infancy—Juvenile literature.
Classification: LCC QL737.C27 I39 2017 | DDC 599.789—dc23
LC record available at https://lccn.loc.gov/2017046599

Printed in the United States of America

To Our Readers: We have done our best to make sure all website addresses in this book were active and appropriate when we went to press. However, the author and the publisher have no control over and assume no liability for the material available on those websites or on any websites they may link to. Any comments or suggestions can be sent by email to customerservice@enslow.com.

Photos Credits: Cover, p. 1 Steve Bloom/Barcroft Media/Getty Images; pp. 4–23 (background image), 15, 23 (main photos) Chip Somodevilla/Getty Images; pp. 5, 7, 19 Foreverhappy/Shutterstock.com; p. 9 China Photos/Getty Images; p. 11 dangdumrong/Shutterstock.com; p. 13 Mitsuaki Iwago/Minden Pictures/Getty Images; p. 17 Keren Su/China Span/Getty Images; p. 21 Steve Bloom Images/Alamy Stock Photo.